AUSTRALIAN
Outback Poems
PHILIP R. RUSH

To my wife, Yvonne, who reads every poem I write, (a sacrifice indeed!) and gives her honest and constructive criticism on each one, a valuable aid to my endeavours.

A very special thanks to Viv Roberts who gave of her time to edit the complete collection of poems in this book,and did it expertly, as usual!

By the same author

Bess, The Black Orpington Swaggie
Australian Poems That Would Stun A Sheep
More Than Nine Lives
Australian Poems That Would Boggle A Bull
Tales from Mosquito Gully and Other Australian Poems
Australian Poems that would Flummox a Farmer
Aussie Poems for Gnome and Garden
Australian Poems that would Dazzle a Dingo
Australian High Country Poems

Published by Philip R. Rush Pty. Ltd.   A.C.N. 082 969 882
224 Sunny Hills Road
Glen Huon Tasmania 7109

1st Edition   March 2002   6000 copies

Printed and bound by The Monotone Art Printers Pty Ltd.
Argyle Street, Hobart Tasmania

ISBN 0 9585443 9 5

CONTENTS

THE OUTBACK

('THE OUTBACK' is a well-known term to all Australians, and each of us has a slightly different understanding of what constitutes 'THE OUTBACK'; where are its boundaries, and is it just an area of land somewhere in Australia, or is there something more to it? This poem, only one of two in this book which have been published previously, first appeared in my fifth book of poetry 'Australian Poems That Would Flummox A Farmer',and is my attempt to try and give some definition to the term 'THE OUTBACK'. Feel free to disagree with me!)

The Outback! Where's the Outback? Is it somewhere back of
     Bourke?
Or where the pioneers did their pioneering work?
Is it out beyond the Darling? Or out past Uluru?
Or is it where it never rains, and skies are always blue?

Some find it in the gibber where the summer heat's intense;
Some find it on the treeless plains beyond the dingo fence,
Or through the Simpson Desert where the sand is never still,
Where the loneliness and silence can daunt the stoutest will.

I've found it west of Broken Hill, and south of Longreach, too,
Where coolibah and gidyea grow beside the great Barcoo.
I've found it in the Flinders where the creeks so rarely run,
Where the mountains are a picture as they watch the winter sun.

Now all of these are places, and I'm sure it's true to say
That they all reflect the Outback, and will for many a day.
But the Outback's more than places, more than things to go and
        see.
It's a quality or essence in the heart of you and me.

The Outback features highly in the spirit of our land;
It's more than distant mountains, it's more than drifting sand.
You'll find it in our history, in the lives of many a bloke,
In our swaggies, drovers, stockmen, and the hardy womenfolk.

You cannot grasp the Outback, not completely, anyway,
For its spirit is elusive in a most frustrating way.
You can sense the Outback's presence, you can know that's where
        you are,
Whether in the streets of Melbourne, or east of Marble Bar.

You can journey to the Outback in an actual literal sense,
Smell the scent of desert breezes, touch the ancient dingo fence;
But that isn't what the Outback ever was, or isn't now,
It is in part, for certain, but it's more than that, somehow.

The intangible component, the very heart and soul
Is needed to be present to make the Outback whole.
And the spirit of the Outback can be partly felt and heard
In the writings of our poets as they share the written word.

The Outback isn't only in the great beyond "out there",
For the spirit of the Outback is for all of us to share.
It pulses through our history with a never-ending beat,
From the ranges west of Alice to the cold, suburban street.

When the situation's trying and the circumstances tough;
When life is full of problems and the going's looking rough,
We see the Outback surface in a man's laconic grin,
In the psyche of the battler who refuses to give in.

The Outback is the mettle, it's the steel within us all;
We feel its distant drumbeat, and we hear its tireless call.
There is an actual Outback, but it's only seen in part,
For the spirit of the Outback is within the nation's heart!

THE OLD-TIMER

(Many and varied are the people we meet as we travel around this great country of ours. Some we meet in reality, some we meet in our imagination, and some are a mixture of both. Who this fellow was is for you to determine!)

His face was carved like the craggy cliffs as the weight of years he
    wore,
And his hair stood white as the breaking waves on a wild
    Australian shore.
His deep-set eyes were the faded blue of the Outback's summer
    sky,
And his hands were gnarled as a twisted gum, and he paused ere
    he passed me by.

He wore his age in his face and hands, and his name I don't recall,
But he said "G'day," with a friendly smile, as he spoke with a lazy
    drawl.
We stood and talked for a moment or two out there in the dusty
    street
Before he said, "Let's go to the pub away from this wretched
    heat!"

"That sounds a good idea," I said, for I'd little enough to do;
So we sat in the pub at a table there and shared in a drink or two.
But I didn't speak very much at all, for he told of days gone by,
And, as he did, I was quite convinced there were tears in his
    ageing eyes.

He spoke of times in the desert sands where the moonless sky
 shone bright,
As the silver gleam of a million stars glowed clear in the
 frozen night.
Of days of dust on the western plains, of flood in the Cooper
 Creek,
Where the restless mob would have to wait for week upon
 weary week!

He told of nights when the dingoes howled, and the outback folk
 he knew;
He told of the endless gidyea scrub far out by the great Barcoo.
He told of sheds where thirty blokes would shear for a month
 or more,
Of hunting pigs in the Queensland bush, and facing an angry
 boar.

It was getting close to closing time when up he rose from his
 seat,
And stood with a long and pensive look on his rather unsteady
 feet,
"So long," he said, as he walked to the door, "So long to you,
 my lad."
And, as he left, I have to admit, I felt just a trifle sad.

He was, of all the people I'd met, the most interesting of men;
But this bloke I'd met in the empty street, I never would meet
 again.
He brought to life the way things were in our history's earlier
 day;
But what had made me a little sad was the bill he left me to
 pay!

OUTBACK NAMES

(There are many wonderful names in the outback: place names, names of stations, names of rivers, mountains and deserts - here are a few of my favourites!)

Innamincka, Ernabella, Parachilna, Uluru,
Oodnadatta, Matarinka, Andamooka, Yandaroo.
Cameron Corner, Tibooburra, Mungerannie, Isis Downs,
And Bedourie, Birdsville, Blinman - three tiny, isolated towns.

Thargomindah, Bourke, Betoota, Urandangi, Breadalbane,
Eromanga, Cork, Thylungra, and the Mundi Mundi Plain.
Warraweena, Arkaroola, Gidgealpa, Watson's Bore,
Muttaburra, Mooraberree, and there're several thousand more!

The Diamantina and the Thomson, Federal Tank, and Cooper
     Creek,
Mount Edward Graves and Mount Peculiar, and there's
     Ambulginya Peak.
The Olgas, Musgrave, Dulcie, Flinders, the Jarrah Jarrahs and
     Mount Dare,
The Simpson and the Tanami deserts, sand and gibber everywhere!

Blueshirt Dam, Corella River, Paddy's Bore and Pigeon Lake,
Nick o'Time Bore and Bulloo River, and Jam Tin Yard, for
     goodness sake!
Bamboo Swamp and Pollygammon, Uwinya Hill and Emu
     Bluff,
Nearly sixty names I've listed, and, I think, that's quite enough!

STREAK - FOREVER FAITHFUL

(Camels and camel drivers were both a common sight and a necessary adjunct in the life of 'The Centre' from the mid eighteen sixties until they were displaced by the introduction of the motor truck. There were still some commercial camel teams as late as the nineteen thirties and forties, but their days were numbered.
Many stories were told of their exploits, and many tales, both true and otherwise, were shared around countless camp fires. This is one of them.)

He was a camel driver in the outback desert region
Back in the nineteen twenties, or somewhere thereabout;
And the stories told about him are colourful and legion,
But are mostly hint and rumour, with little truth, no doubt!

What name this fellow went by is lost in history's pages,
Buried in the endless sandhills somewhere south of Cooper
    Creek.
But he'd been a camel-driver for what, it seemed, was ages,
And he had a heeler with him that was known to all as 'Streak'.

Now Streak was not a puppy, and his pedigree was dubious,
There was surely heeler in him, but some other breeds beside:
Some collie and some kelpie, and his temper fast and furious,
There was nought he wouldn't tackle, he'd take trouble in his
    stride!

He was used to mobs of cattle - he'd belonged to some old
      drover,
And time was well against him, for he now could scarcely
      run;
But the camel driver's days were also getting close to over,
So they aged in years together like the setting of the sun.

Yet, regardless of his temper, Streak was faithful beyond
      measure;
He never left his master's side, he was his closest friend.
And the camel-driving fellow thought his dog his greatest
      treasure,
A partnership so wondrous that you'd wish it wouldn't end.

It was in a little shanty that the dog and man together
Lived out each morn and evening on the outskirts of the town.
Then, one day in late December in the summer's fiercest
      weather,
Someone noticed they were missing, so they tried to track them
      down.

The bloke still owned a camel, so they thought he might have
      followed
His camel through the sandhills, for it often strayed away.
They searched for near a fortnight, round each sand dune and
      each hollow,
But no sign of dog or driver, though they searched both night
      and day!

It was several years later when a stockman was out riding,
As he searched for station cattle, noticed on a sandy flat
What seemed to be a skeleton; he took some time deciding
Whether he would keep on going, or take a look at that!

But curiosity entrapped him, and he slowly wandered over
Where whitened bones lay shining upon the desert sand;
And the skeleton he reckoned was of some forgotten drover,
Who had been another victim of our unforgiving land!

The response he found surprising when he showed what he'd
    discovered
To others on the station somewhat later in the week.
"Hey! He's the camel driver!" And the mystery was
    uncovered,
For lying on the body was the skeleton of Streak!

FREDERICK WILLIAM HARRISON
HARROWSMITH-CLARK

(Over the past one hundred and fifty years, many people have 'headed west' to seek their fortune. Some became famous for their skill and tenacity in raising stock , for example, Sir Sidney Kidman, Sir Thomas Elder, the Duracks and MacDonalds spring readily to mind; others became well-known for their droving skills,and Nat Buchanan, Bill Gwydir, and Matt Savage are noted examples. Others gained fame as cattle duffers (Harry Redford), bushmen and horsemen (R.M. Williams, Lance Skuthorpe and Charlie Philpott), explorers, surveyors, and many other things.
Many, however, did not become famous, and their histories are lost somewhere in the dunes and deserts, saltbush plains and gidyea scrub of the great Outback. This poem is a tribute to the forgotten ones - those who helped develop the land, but who are now not even memories.
'Frederick William Harrison Harrowsmith-Clark' is a poem, not about any individual for, as far as I know, no such person ever existed; however, it is a story that 'could have been', and there were probably many folk who fit part of the picture that is painted in the following verses.)

He left his native Somerset in eighteen eighty-three,
And, looking for adventure, he sailed across the sea.
His father was a titled man, and very wealthy, too,
He said, "You have my blessing, son; my sole advice to you
Is never speak or act in ways that brings you any shame,
For there's value quite immeasurable in one's respected name.
Goodbye, my son, and don't forget, wherever you may roam,
To keep in touch with those of us who still remain at home."

The son bade all a fond farewell, and started on his trip;
He headed for Australia on a mighty clipper ship.
It was to Sydney Town he came and went to step ashore,
But was stopped by some official with a sergeant-major's roar.
"I have to have your name, my lad, before you disembark!"
"It's Frederick William Harrison Harrowsmith-Clark."

He didn't stay in Sydney Town, he thought he'd try his hand
At working on the stations in Australia's hinterland.
He bought a horse and headed west, working as he went,
And many different jobs he did, this youthful English gent.
From drover, stockman, fencing work, from cook to jackeroo,
There wasn't any outback work this fellow wouldn't do.
He so impressed the station bosses they each asked him to stay,
But every time his answer was, "I must be on my way.
There's more for me to see and learn." And he'd head further out,
Until he struck the Barcoo plains and thought he'd stick about.
Every bloke who worked with him would call him 'Pommy Fred',
And he would smile good naturedly and slightly tilt his head.
But, whenever someone asked his name, he always would remark,
"It's Frederick William Harrison Harrowsmith-Clark."

He worked a year, or thereabouts, around the great Barcoo,
At Isis Downs, and Portland Downs, and other stations, too.
He sometimes ventured to the pub, but never spent his cheque;
He'd only have a drink or two - not be a drunken wreck!
One night, at Isisford it was, a shearer's cook was there,
And, going to the English chap, began to curse and swear.
"You filthy, Pommy immigrant, you're all the stinkin' same."
And more expletives foul he used to slander Freddie's name.
"Come outside, you rotten Pommy, I'll show you how to fight!"
He put his fists up to his face, but Pommy Fred sat tight.

The shearer's cook then swung a punch, and threw a wooden
    stool,
But Frederick, with a single blow, laid out the silly fool.
With ease he carried him outside and dropped him in the dark,
Did Frederick William Harrison Harrowsmith-Clark.

He stayed beyond the time he set around these western plains,
Deciding that he'd stay and work until the summer rains.
Whether working as a jackeroo, or shearing in a shed,
Or stockman in the gidyea scrub, his reputation spread.
An ageing station owner who was getting past his prime,
Asked Fred to be his manager, if he could spare the time.
His answer was affirmative, and, for a year or two,
He managed half-a-million acres out west of the Barcoo.
He ran it so successfully his boss asked him to stay
While he took his wife and daughter for a lengthy holiday.
But he was never to return; in Brisbane Town he died,
With both his wife and daughter sitting, grieving, by his side.
So who remained as manager of Mungobilly Park?
Frederick William Harrison Harrowsmith-Clark.

For several months in Brisbane Town the wife and daughter stayed,
Whilst, back at home, the manager his station skills displayed.
The stockmen, cook, and jackeroos, he managed all the staff,
He ran the property aright upon the folks' behalf.
And when, at last, they both returned to their far western home,
Young Pommy Fred decided, too, he would no longer roam;
For he had fallen deep in love, and he had missed the most
The daughter of his widow boss, while both were on the coast.

He courted her with English grace, with noble words and charm,
He courted her for quite a while upon the outback farm.
At last his courting had results, and she became his wife,
And there they lived together the remainder of their life.
The two of them became renowned, a family of mark,
The Frederick William Harrison Harrowsmith-Clarks!

Two bonnie boys were born to them, I think their Christian names
Were Frederick Peter Adamson and William Maxwell James.
They grew up strong and healthy, and, as tradition rules,
Were sent, at tender years of age, to fancy boarding schools.
They'd come back home in holidays, enjoyed it fairly well,
But weren't that keen on station life, as far as I can tell.
Still, Pommy Fred had hopes for them, and thought his children
        may
Take on the station after him - inherit it one day.
And so he worked and persevered through years of flood and
        drought:
The dry of nineteen two and three near had him down and out!
The shearers' strike of ninety-three had been a problem, too,
But, like each flood and searing drought, he managed to get
        through!
And so he most successfully ran Mungobilly Park,
Did Frederick William Harrison Harrowsmith-Clark.

As seasons came and seasons went, the station thrived and grew;
And Frederick took a trip back home, and took his family, too.
But, having no desire to stay - he missed the endless plain,
He made a soon and safe return, and never left again.
What best he liked was mustering, and riding round his place,
He loved the vastness of the scrub, the open plains and space.

But then across the nation wide were heard the storms of war,
And both his boys enlisted like so many had before.
He found their parting difficult, but told his boys the same
As what his father said to him, "Don't soil the family's name:
Do what you have to do, my sons, and do it to your best -
And write to us." Then both his wife and Pommy Fred, distressed,
Watched them ride away from home, for Europe to embark:
Their offspring, Frederick Junior and Maxwell Harrowsmith-
  Clark.

The boys were kept together, and both were sent to France,
But war has no respect for life, survival's left to chance.
The boys were victims of the guns which sent their lethal rounds,
And both their lives were sacrificed on France's battlegrounds.
Many bitter tears were shed by Frederick and his wife,
Who, like parents nation wide, grieved at the loss of life
Of many of Australia's sons who each had heard the call
From friends in need, and went to war, in foreign lands to fall.
Although they lived for many years, the loss of both their boys
Had, understandably, reduced the things that brought them joy.
And when they both grew old and frail, and then in tombs were
  laid,
The station was by neighbours bought; the homestead soon
  decayed.
No history's left, or ruins remain of Mungobilly Park,
Or Frederick William Harrison Harrowsmith-Clark.

A CUP OF TEA

(There is nothing that can compare with a cup of tea - and this is especially so when one is travelling through the vast distances of the Australian bush. To sit beside a billabong or mountain tarn, or on a beach somewhere along Australia's enormous coastline and enjoy a cup of tea is one of life's great pleasures.
This poem reflects that joy!)

I've drunk a mug of tea beside the Mundi-Mundi Plain,
As the sun lit up the evening with a glorious refrain
Of gold and pink and orange, with a hint of pearly grey;
A magnificent conclusion to a marvellous outback day!

I've boiled my battered billy in the Flinders Ranges, too,
Where the hills are red and ochrous, and the sky a brilliant blue.
Where ubiquitous corellas, in the evening's fading light,
Screech and squabble in the gum trees as they settle for the night.

I've sat beneath a she-oak and I've drunk my cup of tea
Beside the Barcoo River with a book upon my knee;
And the springtime breezes sighing in the branches overhead,
While the golden perch lie hiding on the muddy river bed.

I've headed west from Rockie to unique Carnarvon Gorge,
Where the summer heat reminds you of a smithy's fiery forge.
I've waded in the shallows, sat on the sandy banks,
And drunk my sweetened cuppa with a word or two of thanks.

I've sat amongst the saltbush by a dusty, inland track,
With a mob of 'roos beside me and the sun upon my back.
And, as I've sat there resting with my thermos mug of tea,
Sometimes a group of emus come to have a look at me!

On Tasmanian Western Arthurs where all is wet and wild,
Where the wilderness is rampant, and completely undefiled.
Where the shouts of mountain giants crash their echoes in dissent,
I've enjoyed a warming cuppa from the safety of my tent.

I've drunk tea at Mallacoota, and on Mount Buffalo,
And high on the Monaro with the paddocks under snow.
I've even drunk a cuppa on the islands of Bass Strait,
But there's nothing beats the billy by a camp fire with a mate!

PODDY-DODGER'S BAR

('The Dinkum Dictionary' by Lenie Johansen, defines poddy -dodger as a 'person who steals, poaches unbranded calves', in other words, a cattle-duffer. Harry Redwood, or Captain Starlight as he was known, was one of Australia's most famous rustlers.
At Wilpena Pound Resort, in the Flinders Ranges, his fame is remembered in the naming of one of the rooms as 'Poddy-Dodger's Bar' and, next to it, 'Captain Starlight's Room'.
This poem tells of Harry Redford's most famous exploit, along with the resultant trial - and its unexpected outcome!)

We're here at Poddy-Dodger's next to Captain Starlight's room,
A name well known to most of us from history's dusty gloom.
Back in the eighteen eighties he had no claim to fame,
Just a small-time Queensland farmer, Harry Redford was his
      name.

He lived in Wombunderry, that's what he called his place;
A farm that's disappeared, I think, completely without trace.
To stock his farm with cattle he worked for Bowen Downs,
Carting goods with horse and wagon from the rail at Tambo
      Town.

The Gympie gold rush, so I'm told, had also started then,
And cattle-station owners lost a huge amount of men;
For many sought their fortune in the goldfields to the east,
So there weren't sufficient workers to guard the graziers' beasts.

Harry Redford and his cronies thought they could easily make
A fortune duffing cattle - down the Cooper they could take
A mob of many hundreds from the station, Bowen Downs,
And sell them off in Adelaide for several thousand pounds.

In March of eighteen seventy the mustering began,
All done in stealth and secrecy as only rustlers can.
I've seen the yards they specially built to put them in that
   year,
Up on the Thompson River, a long way north of here.

Five men left Balaclava with near a thousand head,
Including, too, a massive bull, completely white, it's said.
They drove them down the Thompson till they reached the
   famed Barcoo,
Where James McPherson left them, as did McKenzie, too.

This left just three of them to push the cattle down the line,
And this they did until, in June, they reached Wallelderdine.
They there convinced the manager that they were fair and
   square,
And sold the white bull to him, and continued on from there.

They pushed for several hundred miles along the pastured
   track,
And no intention did they have of ever turning back!
They came, at last, to Elder's place, the great Blanchewater
   Station,
Where Captain Starlight, as he's known, did the negotiation.

Five thousand pound for all the stock, a princely sum back then,
Enough for many years, I'd say, for Starlight and his men.
To Adelaide went Harry with the other two in tow;
But what then happened to his mates I guess we'll never know.

The two that left him earlier decided to attest
To what they'd all been up to - in other words, confessed!
And so the search for Starlight began in earnest then,
For he'd been put right in it by the two remaining men.

They arrested him in February of eighteen seventy-two;
In New South Wales they found him, but his local stature grew,
For the townsfolk back in Queensland were not the squatters'
        friends,
And they worked a little miracle to, somehow, make amends.

The blokes who'd bought the cattle were summoned to the
        Court,
And damning evidence they gave, or so the Counsel thought.
But no defence gave Starlight; the judge, in his summation,
Said the case against was watertight, in his own estimation.

At eight o'clock that evening the jurymen retired,
And returned a little later, as they had been required.
Judge Blakeney asked their verdict, "Not guilty," they replied.
So he asked again, for justice he knew had been denied.

"Not guilty!" came the answer; the judge went pink, then blue,
But they'd pronounced their verdict, and nothing could he do.
Not even give to Harry a reprimand or fine,
"Thank God that verdict's yours," he said, "and, gentlemen,
        not mine!"

The courtroom had been crowded, and everybody cheered;
Their hero had no sentence, their hero had been cleared.
So Harry, Captain Starlight, was a legend in his time;
But I have just a little more to finish off this rhyme.

There're some would say he brought the mob into Wilpena
        Pound,*
A story, so I'm sharply told, does not hold any ground.
But if you wish to think he did, if that tale you attracts,
Don't let a story that you like be compromised by facts!

*This verse is added because I first performed this poem in 'Poddy-
Dodger's Bar' at Wilpena Pound Resort - August 2001.

HANDY ANDY!

(Some fellows can do everything! Andy is such a bloke!)

There's nothing Andy cannot do,
From cooking bread to Irish stew.
Ride a bull in the holding yard,
Always hold the winning card.
He shears two hundred sheep a day,
And musters every wandering stray.
He's swum the Cooper Creek in flood,
Pushed bullocks through three feet of mud.
And Andy always can, of course,
Break in the wildest, mongrel horse!
He drinks a dozen pots a night,
And wakes up early, feeling bright!
He's never lost a fight at all
In even the fiercest bar-room brawl!
And shoot! Well! He a 'roo can slay
From close on half a mile away!
There is no place he hasn't been,
From Perth to London - met the Queen!
Tibet, Alaska, France, Nepal,
He has visited them all.
And he is quite a genius, too,
Knows the encyclopaedia through.
Tallest mountains, longest streams;
He even can interpret dreams!
How do we know all this is true,
About all this that he can do?
About the genius that he is,
And all this travelling of his?
We're sure it's true - all this we know,
For he, himself, has told us so!

TERRA NULLIUS

(Australia's original inhabitants, the aborigines, have been treated, for the most part, harshly and unfairly over the two centuries of European settlement, and I, amongst thousands of others, am sorry for what has occurred over that period of time.

The first white men to come declared the land 'terra nullius' - an empty land, uninhabited, which, of course, wasn't true. Some slight redress has occurred over recent years, notably the 'Mabo' decision, where the claim for land title by a small community, led by Eddie Mabo, was upheld in Australia's High Court.

The aborigines, our indigenous brothers and sisters, have a great affinity to the land, and a strong claim to areas throughout our nation. May justice be given in the years to come.

I first shared this poem at a poetry reading in Sydney, soon after the Mabo decision had been handed down. I was pleased to be able to share that night with Kerry Reed-Gilbert, an aboriginal poet whose poetry spoke powerfully to those of us who were fortunate enough to be there to hear her.)

An empty land, a vacant land, unpeopled, uninhabited;
No fox, no sparrow, goat or horse, uncamelled and unrabbited.
And then the white man came and stayed, and lived their
     meagre history,
Not recognising those before, whose origin is mystery.
The aboriginal, the black, was not considered one of us,
And so the land was thus declared unpeopled - 'terra nullius'.

The aboriginal is lost when they are dispossessed of land,
For their existence, heart and soul, is bound in rock and earth and
   sand.
Two centuries on, their Dreaming fades, their fire of hope now but
   a spark,
But then a judgment handed down revives the flame and shed
   the dark.

For court of law has now proclaimed that 'terra nullius' is wrong:
The aboriginal has rights to where he's dwelt for ages long.
"To use, possess and occupy, to once again enjoy the land,"
From which, for twenty decades long, he has been so unjustly
   banned.

TWO GRANDSONS

*(As Kerry and I shared together, we discovered that we each had a
grandson two years of age - hence this poem.)*

Two little boys, both two years of age,
Two little Australians beginning life's page.
One of them white and one of them black,
Maybe they'll meet some years down the track.
And when, if they do, I trust that they'll find
Attitudes then of a different kind.
Attitudes friendly, and attitudes new,
Attitudes saying, "We're equal, us two."
"I'm glad you're a person, a person like me,
 Our skin and our race don't matter, you see.
We're two grand Australians, that's where it should end;
Let's walk through the future together as friends."

WILL MACDONALD

(There are hundreds of stories about the exploits of our pioneers and the hardships they suffered. Some of the greatest exploits were the cattle drives - and the longest stock drive ever undertaken in Australia was one of three thousand five hundred miles by the MacDonald brothers and their cousins, the Mackenzies. Only Will MacDonald completed the drive from Goulburn to the West Kimberleys, where he then established Fossil Downs Station in eighteen eighty-six, and it is still owned by the MacDonald family. This poem is the story of that cattle drive.)

If ever a man deserved renown,
It was Will MacDonald of Fossil Downs.
For in eighty-six, in the month of June,
After braving drought and the long monsoon,
After struggling just to stay alive,
He completed the longest cattle drive
That a man has ever undertaken,
If our history books are not mistaken.
Without his friends, who had died or left,
He finished his trek, alone, bereft,
Except for his cook, and a stockman, too,
Who joined him late on his journey through.

The explorer, Forrest, had found the best
Of the pastoral lands in the far north-west.
He reported back to the powers that be
On the wondrous land that was there to see.
With plenty of grass, and running streams,
It answered many a grazier's dreams.

The MacDonalds also received a note,
And were pleased with what the explorer wrote
About these lands in the western state,
And sent one son to investigate.
By what he saw he was most impressed,
So the family decided to head out west.

Their cousins, too, the MacKenzie clan,
Became a part of MacDonalds' plan.
But, just before they were due to go,
The party suffered a dreadful blow.
MacDonald Senior, unluckily, died,
Thrown from his horse on a morning ride.
Some took his death as a warning sign,
And cautiously chose to stay behind.
But the rest determined to carry on;
And, by autumn in eighty-three, were gone.
Gone from their homes near Goulburn Town,
To take up their lease at Fossil Downs.

Of stock they had seven hundred head,
With fifty horses, I've heard it said.
And to help them all fulfil their dreams,
They drove a couple of bullock teams
That pulled two wagons equipped with stores,
As they headed east for Sydney's shores.
From Sydney a trail to Bourke they traced,
Whereat the sobering news they faced
That further north was a fearsome drought,
So more of the party opted out.
Only seven left for the Queensland border
To keep the hungry mob in order.

Bad news they heard at the Queensland gate,
A tax was imposed by the northern state
To discourage the drovers coming in,
For the rivers were low, and the pastures thin.
The MacDonalds weren't ones for turning back;
They continued walking the dusty track.
But, with water scarce, and paddocks bare,
They were met with many a stony glare:
For the local blokes were hard-pressed, too,
And hated the drovers passing through.
But a few of the farmers helped them out
As best they could, in the wretched drought.

Six months they'd been on the weary road,
And the lack of feed for the cattle showed.
There were others, too, on the track out west,
And all of them knew they would have to rest.
No chance, in the drought, to reach their goal,
They camped at Parapitcherie Waterhole,
With the Duracks and Nat Buchanan, as well.
And Costello, too, shared the long, dry spell
Which continued for months; and cattle died.
The MacKenzies, sadly, prepared to ride,
For they'd decided to go back home,
And leave the MacDonalds on their own.

Month after weary month went by,
And still no clouds in the northern sky.
Donald and Charlie and brother Will,
Were camped at Parapitcherie still.

And when, at last, the rains arrived,
They couldn't restart their cattle drive.
For their stock was weak, and the numbers low,
And the three agreed that, before they'd go,
Wherever they could they would take a job
To build up the now depleted mob.
And not until late in eighty-four,
Were the brothers three on the road once more.

North to the Gulf across flooded plain,
They drove their mob to the west again.
Through crocodile-infested flats,
And plagued by clouds of biting gnats,
They battled on, but with little luck,
For, near the border, disaster struck.
Unbeknown to them, they'd been watched for days,
As they made their way through the scrubby maze.
The frightened blacks didn't understand
Why the white men walked on their tribal land.
And they caused the mob to be put to flight,
By spearing a few in the dead of night.

When the stock had gone, and the night lay still,
Donald and Charlie and brother Will
Kept anxious watch with their loaded guns,
Till the sky was red with the morning sun.
They found their mob in the steaming dawn,
With blood-stained hides, and with broken horn.
They were on the move again by noon,
And limped their beasts to the next lagoon.

But wherever they camped, by rivers or creeks,
The cattle were nervous at night for weeks.
The brothers, at last, watched the mob relax;
But were struck again by the local blacks.

It was thirty months on the lonesome road,
With their cattle and horses, and wagonload;
Thirty long months when this stoic band
Pushed their way into Arnhem Land
But mosquito-infested waterholes
Took an ever-increasing toll
On the brothers three: they were taken ill,
But made for Kimberley country still.
Then, with a thousand miles to cross,
A wagon broke down, a disastrous loss!
The Roper River brought a further curse,
For Charlie's fever was undoubtedly worse.

Will spoke to Don, they were in some strife,
And they feared for their brother Charlie's life.
"We haven't a choice, he'll need you, Don,
To see he gets safe to Palmerston.
And I bet you a quid to a hundred pounds
That I'll beat you both to Fossil Downs."
Alone, each day he would ride out west,
And sought a path that would suit him best.
Then back he'd come for his trusty cart,
See to the cattle, and then depart
To the camp he'd chosen - and then, again,
Ride back for his mob on the northern plain.

Willie MacDonald, a courageous man,
For months continued his three-stage plan.
Ride on alone, then back for the cart,
Then again for the herd - it'd break one's heart
To see his haggard and bearded frame,
Gaunt with fever and racked with pain,
Sitting straight and proud, as he made his course,
On his tried and true long-suffering horse.
Over the border, and short of stores,
He turned his mob to the northern shores;
And there, at Wyndham, a stockman found,
Who accompanied him on the final round.

Through dust and heat and swarming flies,
They arrived at Derby, and bought supplies.
Then, turning east, they made their way
To Fossil Downs, to stop and stay.
Three-seventy head, and a horse or two
Were all of the stock that made it through.
But the epic journey that Will completed
Has never been matched, and never repeated.
There're few now, if any, knew Will alive,
But many remember his cattle drive.
And if ever a man deserved renown,
It was Willie MacDonald of Fossil Downs!

THE WATERHOLE AT EVENING

*(There is nothing more welcome in the desert country of outback
Australia than a waterhole, especially if it has permanent water.
Surrounded by coolibah trees, ghost gums and a variety of smaller
trees and shrubs, along with a sprinkling of native grasses, the
desert waterhole is a haven for the desert birds and animals, and
the weary traveller!)*

The trees are silhouetted against a brassy sky,
And a zephyr blows unfettered as it gently whispers by.
It's come from dune and gibber, from country stark and bare,
And the faint, sweet smell of desert lingers in the drifting air.

The searing heat is easing as the evening softly falls,
And, in the reed bed hiding, the secret bittern calls.
One hears the cheerful chatter of the froglets as they wake,
And, perhaps, the haunting chirring of a little water crake.

The desert loses colour in the quickly fading light,
And corellas squawk and squabble as they settle for the night.
The galahs are calling harshly as they flash their pink and grey
Above the splendid ghost gums at the ebbing of the day.

As the shade of twilight thickens, the creatures come to drink
From their burrows and their shelters beside the desert brink.
They come with care and caution, with timidity, at first,
But become somewhat emboldened as they satiate their thirst.

The deepening night is softened by the moonlight's gentle
        beam
Which reflects upon the ripples in a scintillating stream.
And a million stars in heaven, each one a silver spark,
Lift the heavy veil of blackness as they glimmer in the dark.

As time meanders slowly through the stretches of the night,
The solitude and stillness bring a sensuous delight.
As the whispers of the evening and all murmurations cease,
The world is bathed in silence, and the desert is at peace.

OLD JESS

(Dogs are an integral part of station life, and good sheep or cattle dogs are worth their weight in gold! But, like ourselves, dogs age and, also like us, retirement doesn't always come easy. Such is the case with old Jess, a dog I have known since her youth.)

Old Jess, what a marvellous dog she's been!
With her collie coat, and her body lean.
She's built for work, and she's cheerfully done
Her assignments well in the summer sun;
In the winter's chill, and the autumn gale,
Not once have we ever seen her fail!

In the open paddock, the road or yard,
Old Jess would be always working hard;
Controlling sheep with a bark or nip,
Or a threatening growl through a curling lip.
Not a ewe or a ram had the slightest chance
To escape from Jess with her watchful stance.

She'd sit on the bike, or the open tray
Of the ute, on a typical working day,
Until we spoke a commanding word,
Or she a short, sharp whistle heard;
Then off in a flash with a spring-heeled leap,
Delighted to muster the startled sheep.

Her casts were wide, and her senses keen,
And rarely a better dog we'd seen.
Her fitness, too, was second to none,
For she never tired, all day she'd run
With the easy lope that would see her through
Whatever the task she was asked to do.

But now she's old, and her muzzle's grey;
She's not as sprightly as yesterday.
No longer she'll jump from a standing start
Up onto the ute, and we've not the heart
To see her struggle, so we help her up,
Which she'd refuse when a lively pup.

She loves to work in the paddock still,
But, nowadays, when she's had her fill,
She'll rest awhile in a patch of shade,
And not all orders are now obeyed.
For now old Jess doesn't hear too well,
Or decides she won't! - It's hard to tell.

She's nobody's fool, and, just of late,
She's learnt to open the house-yard gate.
She comes and she goes as she likes, does Jess,
But she won't cause any harm, I guess.
She's rising twelve, or somewhat more,
And she's not much mischief left, I'm sure!

Another year or two, I'd say,
Will see Jess rest on a working day.
She'll let the others go mustering sheep,
While staying behind for a well-earned sleep.
And there in a patch of sun she'll lie,
Contentedly dreaming of days gone by!

THE SPIRIT OF MATILDA

*(This is the second of only two poems in this book which have been
published previously. It was written by request some years ago,
and expresses some of my thoughts about "Waltzing Matilda,"
which has a special meaning to many of us.
We like to think we have a close connection to our outback history,
our pioneering past. Even those born in the depths of the great
Australian cities often feel a deep affinity with the rugged, dry
interior of our land, and with the struggle many of our forebears
had as they tried to set up home in the vast emptiness of our country.
There is also an independence in the Australian character that
gives many of us a {healthy?} suspicion of authority!)*

He may have been a vagabond, a rogue, or petty thief,
And may have worked occasionally by way of light relief,
But Banjo's famous swaggie is an Aussie figure grand,
The quintessential battler of our great and wondrous land.

A man content with life he was, of independent bent,
Who managed peacefully, alone, no matter where he went.
He cooked and ate a simple fare, he drank his billy's brew;
And, if a jumbuck chanced along, he'd have a bit of stew.

He dressed for comfort, more or less, he was no stylish fop,
He had no permanent address, at night he'd simply stop
Beside a creek or billabong, his swag beneath his head;
Or, during rain and thunderstorms, he'd camp inside a shed.

He kept his distance from the law, he wanted no dispute,
And rarely acted in a way that might bring ill repute.
He'd known the ups and downs of life, and never took a poke
At other chaps' misfortunes - he was a gentle bloke.

When trouble did confront him, at peace beneath a tree,
He felt condemned unfairly by each of troopers three.
He sprang into the water - in moments he was gone,
But the spirit of Matilda eternally lives on.

The ghost of Banjo's swaggie has called from down the years,
Awakening the spirit that was in our pioneers.
Although we're mostly city-bred, we're Aussies through and
        through,
And like to think that we, ourselves, are independent, too.

We dream of days departed, of life upon the Track,
We yearn for simple solitude somewhere away out back.
We hear from distant memories the bush's haunting call;
For the spirit of Matilda is deep within us all.

THE OUTBACK - 2

(Another view of the outback; somewhat different to that on page one. A personal view, and one that has been influenced by varied experiences of inland Australia.)

The harshness of the Outback is reflected in the screech
Of the cockatoos a-crying from their lookout beyond reach.
Or the hoarse and tuneless cawing of the dusty, blackened crows,
As a mob of 'roos lie resting in a heat-induced repose.

One sees the Outback's dryness in the ever-shifting dunes,
And the all-too-common presence of old cattle station ruins;
In the endless stretch of desert, and the plains of gibber stones,
With their grisly collection of both bleached and whitened bones.

There's a fierceness in the Outback in its fiery, summer days,
And the haunting disappointment of the shimmering, desert haze;
In the baked and empty waterholes and dusty river beds,
And the bare and broken mountains of orange, pink and red.

That the Outback is so boundless is obvious by day
As far-distant horizons seem to, strangely, melt away.
And it's even more apparent in the silence of the night,
As the high, eternal heavens shed their ghostly, silver light.

There are mysteries in the Outback that are buried in the sand,
Or hidden in the vastness of this grand, enormous land;
Tales of drovers and explorers lost in this empty place;
And many other travellers disappearing without trace.

There's a Dreaming in the Outback that tells of times long gone,
Of ancient folk still present as the Dreaming lingers on;
Of those whose very being is part of rock and sand,
Of those whose very spirit still occupies the land.

There's a history in the Outback that speaks of spur and whip,
Of horses, drovers, stockmen, of overlanding trips;
Of feats of exploration that defied the sternest test,
Of famous men and women who have long been laid to rest.

There's a challenge in the Outback that shows the best in men,
As they strive against the elements again, and yet again
Against storms and flooding rivers, and years and years of
    drought,
Against fears of one's abilities to see each season out.

There are colours in the Outback that are rich beyond compare,
In the red heart of the desert, in the flowers, bright and fair.
In the clouds of grey and purple as the thunderstorms roll by;
In the stunning, ochred ranges, and the clear, cerulean sky.

There's a beauty in the Outback that's magnificent and wild,
It's rough, tough and tenacious, and, mostly, undefiled,
There's splendour in the mountains, in a worn and rugged way,
And brilliant, flaming sunsets end many an Outback day!

There's a silence in the Outback that is infinitely deep,
Where one can well imagine that Time, himself's, asleep;
Where the quiet calm of evening is a gift one cannot find
In the city streets and suburbs that we've, thankfully, left behind.

There's a calling that's insistent, there's a calling that today
Calls clearly from the Outback in a most compelling way;
Speaks through the timeless mountains, and from the desert sand,
"Come see and feel and wander, and know my spirit grand!"

CHARLIE

(There are some blokes who just can't help themselves! Charlie was one of those, always playing practical jokes at someone else's expense, until.................)

Charlie was a drover, and a good one, too, at that,
And he, of course, would always wear an ancient drover's hat.
A battered old Akubra, with the brim down front and back,
It served him well for years as he worked the Birdsville Track.

He worked with old Bill Gwydir when he first began to drove,
But only once he played a joke on that outstanding cove.
Bill gave him such a lashing with his strong Boss Drover's
      tongue,
Charlie felt that he'd been horsewhipped, or through a mangle
      wrung!

But he was irrepressible with any other crew,
He'd "take the mickey" from them all, and angered quite a few!
He came with us in fifty-five, but we fair knew him then!
So we had planned a joke on him, me and the other men.

The first few days that we were out, well, Charlie had a ball!
He played these stupid pranks on us, he played them on us all!
Childish things they often were, pretend he'd broke his knee;
Or fill a saddlebag with rocks, or salt the billy tea.

We let it go for near a week, and then we talked of snakes.
"King browns are really thick this year, especially near the lakes."
"Oh! No they're not!" said Charlie. "I know the Birdsville well,
There's not that many round at all, as far as I can tell."

"You don't know what you're saying," said another of the crew.
"At Andrewilla Waterhole they're bigger, lad, than you.
Six feet long if they're an inch, and thick as fleas on dogs,
They hide beneath the scrub, they do, and holes and hollow logs."

"Last month, it was," a mate chimed in. "My mate, who was
    asleep,
Found he had one inside his swag, you should have seen him
    leap.
If you get bitten, Charlie boy, you're gone - without a doubt,
Unless you cut where you get bit, and wash the poison out."

And so we talked of snakes for days, until, at last we came
To Andrewilla Waterhole, of Diamantina fame.
For Andrewilla's on a branch of that distinguished stream,
And guarantees good watering for every drover's team.

We watered all the thirsty stock, we filled our waterbags,
We ate a hearty drover's meal, and then unrolled our swags,
I chose to take first watch that night, and, as I went, I said,
"Take care no snakes get in my swag, I'd hate one in my bed."

Charlie took the midnight watch, the one he liked to do;
It usually went from twelve o'clock until a half past two.
We waited till he'd gone a while before our plan we laid,
And reckoned that his jokes would soon be handsomely repaid!

We'd brought with us a rubber snake, an evil-looking beast,
It was quite scaly to the touch, and five feet long, at least!
We poked it into Charlie's swag, then added several spines
About the spot we reckoned that he'd rest his soft behind!

We crept back to our swags again and never said a word,
Pretending not a thing at all had untoward occurred.

When Charlie came and woke up Fred, whose turn it was to take
The fourth and final watch that night, no noises did we make!

It took but just a moment for Charlie then to climb
Into his swag, where he had hoped to have some sleep sublime.
But, quicker still, he left his bed with one almighty leap,
And gave a loud and piercing yell, and then began to weep.

"I'm bit! I'm bit!" he screamed, in pain, "A snake's bit me in
        bed!"
And, in the moonlight, we could see his face was filled with
        dread.
"What can I do?" he yelled again. "It's bitten me behind!"
And we, still lying in our swags, were feeling most unkind.

But soon our sympathy had passed, and we to Charlie said,
"You've got to let the poison out, the snakebite must be bled!"
He ripped his moleskin trousers off, and opened up his knife;
And we could see poor Charlie was afraid he'd lose his life!

He made a cut along the wound about an inch in length,
And raced into the waterhole with his remaining strength.
He sank into the muddy pool and let the red blood run,
Until we thought he'd had enough, and told him what we'd
        done.

He looked incredulous at first, and then he cursed and swore,
"I'll never, in me life again, trust any bloke no more!"
But, much to Charlie's credit, once safe ashore and dried,
And, after a strong mug of tea, he saw the funny side.

It took us half the following day to muster all the stock,
For they had all stampeded when Charlie yelled in shock!
But it had well been worth it, we had the snake to thank,
For Charlie never, from that day, played anyone a prank!

BILL GWYDIR

(There have been many highly-skilled 'Boss Drovers' over the past one hundred and fifty years, but the most famous of those who regularly worked the stock route known as 'The Birdsville Track' was Bill Gwydir.)

You can talk of Nat Buchanan as a drover of some note,
And Matt Savage, too, was marvellous so some history fellows
    wrote.
Nat pioneered the stock route that they call the Murranji,
And moved the stock in thousands in conditions that would
    try
The toughest breed of stockmen, and Matt Savage did, as well;
And never better drovers walked our land, so some would tell.
But the Birdsville Track had stockmen who were just as famous,
    too,
And the best of them, Bill Gwydir, was a drover through and
    through.

He was born in Cunnamulla in Queensland's outback west,
And his father was a stockman, who thought it would be best
To take his son a-droving while still a tender lad.
So Bill, when only twelve years old, went droving with his
    dad
Way back in nineteen twenty; and then, in 'twenty-two,
Bill went with drover, Massey Hood, a bloke his father knew.
Bill stayed with him a little while, then worked for other chaps,
And gained a reputation fine, did he, around the traps.

In 'thirty-seven Bill thought it time to venture on his own,
For he, throughout his learning years, had independence shown.
He put a plant together, and quickly had a job,
Taking down the Birdsville Track a large St. Leonard's mob.
And, on that trip, Bill and his team were camped at Blaze's
    Well,
When, just on eight o'clock that night, the weather blew like
    hell!
The thunder roared, the lightning flashed, the dust was gravel
    size,
So there was nothing they could see an inch before their eyes!

It blew till three o'clock that night, a shocking time they had;
Bill never knew, before or since, a dust storm quite as bad!
He reckoned that the mob was gone, all blown or strayed away,
But, in the morning, all were found, not one he lost that day!
And, in the years that followed, he proved to be the best
At droving down the Birdsville Track, a cut above the rest.
He crossed the Cooper Creek in flood in nineteen forty-nine,
A droving feat that few would try, and less complete, you'd
    find.

He did the same the following year, and gained no little fame
Across the nation far and wide, for people heard his name
In broadcasts all about the land that told his epic deeds,
And papers, too, reported them for everyone to read.
But, back in nineteen forty-three he'd made a greater drive,
Where stockmen said he'd never get the cattle through alive!
A drive to take the cattle through shifting dunes of sand
South of the Simpson desert, a desolate, arid land.

From the Northern Territory border he was asked to take the mob
Through miles of desert country, a dreadful, droving job!
Jim Oldfield asked him do it, he had seven hundred head
To take to Mungerannie, "Only Bill will do," he said.
Bill started at Abminga, five hundred miles or more
From Mungerannie Station, and the stock were fairly poor!
The scarcity of water and deficiency of feed
Made the job he had in front of him an awkward one, indeed!

There were stages that he covered that were sand for twenty mile
In that harsh and bitter country, but he drove them on in style!
In treacherous quicksand patches the hungry stock he split
Into smaller mobs for safety; it took a lot of grit
For him to tackle such a task, where others would be lost!
And many dusty creek beds and dried waterholes he crossed.
Eleven weeks in thirsty country the mob he carefully led,
And lost three bullocks only of the seven hundred head.

If you'd ever met Bill Gwydir you'd remember him, all right,
The epitome of drovers, a most impressive sight!
With his rusty leather jacket, and his leather leggings, too,
And tightly fitting gabardines, and open shirt of blue.
He wore a tall and wide-brimmed hat, its crown quite worn
    away;
A cigarette, a "roll-your-own", hung from his lips all day.
His legs were long and slightly bowed, quite naturally, of
    course,
For those who spent a lifetime with their legs across a horse.

His skin was tanned as leather, his eyes were clear and bright,
And sparkled with his earthy wit, which one would hear at
    night
As, round the campfire chatting, he'd tell a tale or two
Of life along the drover's track, and of the blokes he knew.
His speech was slightly husky; he'd a rhythmic turn of phrase,
And just a touch of Irish lilt from, perhaps, his father's days.
He never beat about the bush, straight to the point he came;
And he, like others of his ilk, liked you to do the same!

Bill Gwydir rode the Birdsville Track for forty years, or more,
No drover knew the Track like him, not since, and not before.
He had a stint in Sydney Town, but felt that he would choke.
"City life," he'd mutter, "that's enough to kill a bloke."
He made his three score years and ten, he died in 'eighty-one,
A full and hearty life he'd lived, an honest race he'd run.
You can talk of other drovers, of stockmen you can sing,
But, of drovers on the Birdsville Track, Bill Gwydir was the
    King!

MIRAGE

*(Is it real, or is it not?   Can I believe my eyes at all, when the
desert heat distorts the horizon, and conjures up magical images,
only to then make them vanish in front of me?)*

On this, the hottest of summer days,
A lake appears in the shimmering haze,
A haunting lake on the desert sand,
A taunting call to the weary band
Who've traipsed for hours in the blazing heat,
And rejoice to see the lustrous sheet
Of water on the horizon bare.
But elation turns to bleak despair
As the ephemeral lake is quickly gone,
And another appears much further on.

When the midday sun the saltbush sears,
In the burnished distance there appears
A concrete city, tall and wide,
In this uninhabited countryside.
The buildings reach for the open sky
And the outback traveller can't deny
What his own eyes see on the gibber plain.
Then the city fades, and he seeks in vain
To find the non-existent town
Whose spectral walls have tumbled down.

As the warmth disturbs the outback air,
I see great castles standing there.
And then appears across the sky
A herd of camels flying by.
The camels leave, and a kangaroo
Hops lazily 'cross the distant blue;

And twisted trees materialize
In the heavens before my very eyes!
Mirages daily haunt the track
Of those who travel the great Outback!

WHAT HAVE YOU SEEN?

If what you've seen is the wind-blown sand
As a million dunes drift across the land,
And the vast expanse of a gibber plain
That goes for ever and back again;
The flush of life as the deserts bloom
In the wake of a vagrant, lost monsoon;
The violent rush of a creek in flood,
And the waterholes' dry encrusted mud;
The rust-red rocks in their mystic way
Turn purple at the close of day;
The lightning flash from a brooding sky,
A mob of emus passing by;
The whitened skull of a long-dead beast;
The ancient mountains gnarled and creased:
If all of these things you've seen of late,
You've spent some time in the Outback, mate!

If you've heard the caw of the desert crows
And the roaring wind as a dust-storm blows;
The howl of a dingo close at hand,
The whisperings of the shifting sand;
The rustling faint as the breezes pass,
In the fading light, through the spinifex grass;
The silence deep in the midnight glow
Of the moon on the empty land below;
The creaking call as the eagle flies
Above the plains in the midday skies;
The powerful roll of the thunder boom
In the evening's ever-increasing gloom;
The screech of the cockatoos at dawn,
And, at night, the curlew's cry forlorn:
If you heard all this, and more beside,
You've been travelling Australia's Outback wide.

If you've smelt the joy of a sudden rain
As it spreads its life on a thirsty plain;
The stinking mud of a dying stream,
The brackish smell of the salted steam
Which scolds the land, and a good deal more,
As it gushes out from a boiling bore;
The fume of dust, of sand, of sweat,
The pungent gidyea when it's wet.
The sweet, dry scent of the desert scrub,
The welcome smell of a lonely pub!
If you've experienced all of these,
You've smelt the breath of the Outback breeze!

If you've felt the sting of the raging sand,
With the wind so strong you can hardly stand;
The scorching heat of the desert sun
That cooks the sand till it's overdone;
The freezing night that reaches high
Through to the stars in a frosty sky!
The height and depth of the loneliness
That reaches to utter timelessness,
Or the peace of the evening solitude
That gives a sense of a soul renewed:
If you've felt all that, and you wish for more
Of the sights and sounds of the desert floor;
If you want to sense and to smell again
The heat and sand, and the creeks and rain;
If that's your wish, then I know full well,
You've fallen under the Outback's spell!

THE EXPLORERS

(A brief tribute to those who were among the first white men to explore Australia's hinterland.)

Forrest and Stuart, and Kennedy, too,
Buchanan and Giles, to name but a few;
And Eyre, of course, and Burke and Wills,
And Leichardt, lost in the sand or hills.
Warburton, Sturt, and the Gregory brothers
Explored the land, as did plenty of others.

A hardy, nineteenth-century band,
Whose impressive explorations spanned
From east to west, from north to south,
From mountain range to river's mouth,
By boat or by foot, by camel or horse,
Over dune and desert and watercourse.

No trucks or radios, nor often a map,
Through illness and hardship and many mishap,
They braved the heat, the dust and the sand,
To explore our continent's hinterland.
And, on return, they reported back
On what they'd found in our vast Outback.

But some there were who didn't survive,
For, in desert and heat, they lost their lives,
Succumbing to illness and blinding thirst
Once the Outback climate had done its worst!
And others were lost, and died alone,
Leaving nothing but bleached and whitened bone.

Though all have gone, they're remembered still,
As name of a creek, a river or hill.
From the Birdsville Pub to the back of Bourke,
They're remembered, too, for their daring work.
And so this tribute I write today
To the bold explorers who led the way!

CINDER BLACK, OR COLD AND RAW!

(The reputation of most drover's cooks, and shearer's cooks, for that matter, has always been rather suspect. There were, and are, very good cooks on the Track, but, regardless of their expertise, cooks were usually given a pretty rough time by those they were cooking for. One of the reasons for this may well be something to do with the fellow who is written about in this poem. There is, unhappily, some truth in this story!)

The most important bloke, they say, in every drover's crew,
Is any fellow who can cook a roast or decent stew
But expert cooks have always been a little hard to find,
Which brings, as often is the case, another tale to mind.

We had a job in 'forty eight, along an outback route,
But didn't take our usual cook, we'd given him the boot!
He'd been with us for several months, but we could not ignore
That every meal was cinder black, or else completely raw!

So we enquired about the place for some experienced cook;
And, luckily, or so we thought, we hadn't far to look.
It wasn't very long before a scruffy fellow came
And said, "I've been a shearer's cook, and Joseph is my name."

Joseph, as we quickly found, and each of us recall,
Was not the cleanest bloke around; he rarely washed at all!
He never wore his boots in camp, his feet were always bare,
Except for several layers of grime to match his filthy hair!

He did the cooking well enough, as far as we could tell,
But everything we ate, it seemed, had similar taste and smell!
The johnnie cakes and brownies, the potatoes and the stew,
All smelt and tasted just the same, as did the billy's brew!

We rarely saw him at his work, for we were on the Track,
And he'd reach camp before us all and, naturally, unpack.
Once preparations were complete, the meal was under way;
So all was cooked when we arrived toward the end of day.

But once our stockman, Davy, was feeling rather off,
He had a stinking headache, and a very nasty cough.
We told him that we'd manage, for him to go ahead,
That's when he saw how Joseph the evening meal prepared!

All the food that Joseph cooked was always shaped the same,
No matter what went into it, or what the food was named.
The dumplings, patties, brownies, they all were carefully pressed
Beneath Joe's armpits, left or right, next to his hairy chest.

And Joseph heavily perspired, he sweated like a pig:
Sweat dripped into his cooking, but he didn't care a fig!
It ran into the billy tea from matted whiskers grey,
And so both drink and cooking tasted just the same each day!

We managed to survive the trip, despite Joe's sweaty food;
But, at the end, we paid him off, we didn't think it rude!
We couldn't find another cook, except the one we'd had;
But cinder black, or cold and raw, now didn't taste so bad!

THE FLOOD

(The Outback is a land of extremes - extreme heat, extreme dryness, dust, loneliness, distances, and, on irregular occasions, extreme floods! This tells of the years 1949-50, when the long dry spell of 1948 looked like leading into another major drought. This, after the droughts earlier in the decade, could well have spelt ruin for many of the stations.)

It was late in the year of 'forty-eight, and feed was in short
     supply,
And the natural lakes were sun-baked mud: My hat! but the land
     was dry!
The wind came up and the dust blew in; five storms a week in
     December,
As bad as I've ever seen them, lad, and as bad as most can
     remember!

And our mailman, Tom, on the Birdsville Track, was having a
     tough time, too;
Stuck in the dust almost every day, he was digging the whole way
     through!
And the garden at Mrs Oldfield's place was under a yard of sand;
With nary a sign of a shower of rain right across the Outback
     land!

At last, in the twilight of Christmas Eve, the showers began to
     fall,
It rained for a while; not nearly enough! But better than none at
     all!
The clouds were gone inside of a week, and again the weather
     was dry;
And no clouds were seen for a couple of months in the Outback's
     summer sky.

But then a wandering storm 'got lost' - came drifting in from
      the east,
Its thick, dark clouds hung around the skies, I'd say, for a week, at
      least!
And the rain drummed loud on the iron roofs, and a marvellous
      tune it played!
And it sang a song on the thirsty earth, as it over the inland
      stayed.

The dunes rejoiced as it tumbled down, and so did the black-soil
      plains,
As did the desert and gidyea flats, as they drank their fill of the
      rains.
The gullies and channels rejoiced, as well, they sang as the waters
      ran;
And they filled the dams and the waterholes, the hollows and
      salted pans.

The billabongs filled, and the dry swamps, too; and the rivers
      began to run;
Every silted stream and sandy creek joined in with the teeming
      fun!
They chattered and laughed as they raced along, and they
      overflowed their banks,
And sleeping rivers came back to life and, delightedly, joined
      their ranks.

The Burke and Cottonbush, Wills and King, the Georgina and
      Thompson, too,
The Diamantina and Cooper Creek, the Hamilton and Barcoo;
They all ran deep in their dried-out beds, and they thundered a
      deep refrain,
And the great Outback heard a mighty choir as the waters were
      singing again!

The rain persisted for days on end, and the rivers were soon in
     flood;
And the dusty roads of a week before were now impassable mud!
The floods crept up to the station sheds, and even the homestead
     door,
But the sullen clouds remained above, and the rain continued to
     pour.

The rivers became an inland sea, and the refuse of dry years past
Was washed away by the raging tide, by the waters' surging blast.
Carried away was the drifted sand, the logs and the trees long
     dead;
And the waters scoured the rivers, too, and cleaned out their silted
     beds.

The flood flowed strong in the Cooper Creek, and on much of the
     land beside,
(Even late that year on the Birdsville Track, the Cooper was two
     miles wide.)
It hurried across the scalded flats, through sandhills of pearly
     white,
And on it swept with a gleeful roar - an extraordinary outback
     sight!

Once the floods returned to their bedded streams the land was
     awash with grass!
You could hear the songs that the drovers sang as you watched
     their cattle pass.
They swam the bullocks across the creek, and drove them on to
     Marree,
And a happier band of droving men I'd reckon you'd rarely see!

In nineteen fifty it rained again, phenomenal falls they were,
Twenty-five inches in just three weeks, every stream was again
    a-stir!
The Cooper Creek flowed across the sand till it reached a dry
    Lake Eyre,
And spilt its load on the barren waste, on the thirsty saltpans
    there.

A generation, and more, had passed, since the Cooper had run so
    far,
And few remembered, and less had seen, the creek flow across
    the bar
Of that great depression we call Lake Eyre; and the Diamantina,
    too,
With all of its channels full of the flood, had also broken through.

And hence, with successive rainy years, the rumours began to
    spread:
Lake Eyre was not just a salted waste, but full to the brim, they
    said.
Two million acres of water lay in this vast, ephemeral sea,
And its normally unproductive shores were as green as green
    could be!

The Outback is, as I've said before, a country of great extremes,
Where one knew only the dust and heat, everywhere there were
    flooding streams!
But the dry returns, and the drought persists, with the waterholes
    barely mud,
Till a lost monsoon or a wandering storm produces another flood!

THE EMU

(The emu is one of nature's oddities. A bird that is quite enormous compared to most birds, and with feathers which are unlike almost any other feathers you will see. Not only that, but it is the father emu who hatches the eggs, and rears the family - a strange situation indeed!)

Though many people's favourite bird,
The emu's really quite absurd!
Not beautiful, but rather quaint,
And not what one would call a saint!
Massive size, yet stunted wings,
Feathers like fringed, silken strings;
Cannot fly, but runs at speed,
(Forty miles an hour, at need!)
With paces up to nine feet long,
On solid legs both bare and strong.

The emu has no dulcet call,
He grunts or snorts at one and all.
He has a long, ungainly neck,
And he can give a nasty peck
By using his enormous bill,
(Don't try him, for I know he will!)
And, on each foot, the middle toe
Is huge, and hence a vicious blow
Can be inflicted by this bird
If it is harried or disturbed.

Once all the eggs are laid, the hen
Will rarely touch the eggs again.
She leaves the brooding to her mate,
Who doesn't seem to mind his fate!
He faithfully sits upon the nest,
And rarely takes a well-earned rest.
He broods the eggs for sixty days,
Or thereabouts, and thus displays
Great patience and great fortitude,
Both traits with which he's well endued!

The nest is often in the grass,
And, if you're happening to pass,
Even though an emu's tall,
You mightn't notice it at all,
For when he's sitting on the eggs,
He folds his long and lanky legs,
And keeps his neck and head well down
As he sits low upon the ground.
He looks like drying grass or thatch
Whilst waiting for the eggs to hatch.

The baby chicks are quite a sight,
Boldly streaked with brown and white;
They follow father everywhere,
And he gives good, paternal care,
Protecting them as best he can
From dingo, eagle, fox and man.
For eighteen months the chicks will stay
With father never far away.
It's not until they fully grow
Will they their independence show.

When any hungry emu feeds,
It likes to eat both fruit and seeds;
It will eat many leaves, as well,
And farmers, angrily, will tell
How emus love to come and shop
At their latest cereal crop!
On locust swarms they like to dine,
And caterpillar plagues are fine.
And, if you've something nice to crunch,
They'll come and steal your picnic lunch!

The emu lives throughout our land,
From mountain forest to desert sand;
From coastal scrub to saltbush plain.
They often are the farmers' bane,
Destroying crops with legs immense,
And breaking down the paddock fence.
They target, chiefly, cereal farms,
(And one is on our coat of arms!)
Though not the best of farmers' mates,
I'd let them in *my* paddock gates!

In many books I think you'll find
The emu has been much maligned.
And, in the west, in 'thirty two,
They organised a hunting crew
Who shot a thousand birds, or more,
In what was called 'The Emu War'.
But most of us, I think I'm right,
Find emus an attractive sight.
Yet, even though a favourite bird,
The emu really is absurd!

THE HOMESTEAD RUINS

(As you travel throughout outback Australia, you are often reminded of the history of the region. Old ruins and signs, cemeteries, rusting or decaying implements and machinery - all bring us face to face with history.

In the South Flinders Ranges are the remains of the historic homestead 'Kanyaka'. A thriving sheep station in the mid-nineteenth century, it is now but a ruin of chimneys, broken stone walls and buildings, and an unfloored and unroofed, yet reasonably preserved woolshed.

In its heyday, Kanyaka must have been an impressive sight. In 1864, forty thousand sheep were shorn on Kanyaka Station, but now not one remains, only the decaying ruins of a once thriving community. This scenario is oft repeated throughout the Outback.)

The bell would start them working, and the shed would quickly fill
With the sound of sheep and shearers, and the noise would stay
  until
The shearers stopped for smoko, and the racket would subside
Until their rest was over, and they all went back inside
To continue with the shearing, and they shore them head to head,
To see who'd be the ringer in this nineteenth century shed.

And, when the day was over, there was plenty left to do,
A yarn around the camp fire or sing a song or two.
To share some Aussie mateship, to drink a bit of grog,
Or sit and muse in silence on a wooden stump or log.
Or perhaps a little fishing at the local billabong,
Hoping optimistically a fish might come along!

And, in the homestead proper, the servants would prepare
The food for evening dinner which the family would share
With those who may be visiting; and afterwards, maybe,
They'd retire to the parlour where, whilst sipping on some tea,
They'd hear a short recital from a daughter or a son
Playing on some instrument - an evening of fun!

Or, perhaps, some games were played of cards or dice, I guess,
Or they could play at billiards, or a quiet game of chess.
They might finish off the evening with a final glass of wine,
For many of the homesteads were luxurious and fine.
A little bit of comfort in Australia's heat and sand,
To remind them of old England, their far-off motherland.

Not all the station owners had such a fine abode,
Where the wealth of family fortune so obviously showed.
There were many who were battlers; their houses rather poor,
Simply built of slabs and saplings, with a beaten, earthen floor.
But, whether simple dwellings or mansions built of stone,
There're many now in ruins, unpeopled and alone.

For you cannot tame the Outback, its harsh and arid clime
Means those who wish to live there have a battle all the time.
A war against the elements of drought and sand and heat,
A battle often ending in ignominious defeat.
And the relics of the warfare stand broken and decayed,
Whilst the histories of the families soon very quickly fade.

When you travel through the Outback and you see the tattered shreds
Of a long-forgotten homestead and its worn, skeletal sheds;
Spare a thought for those who settled in those pioneering days,
Where their mobs of sheep and cattle were often wont to graze.
For the ruins send a warning that is foolish to ignore,
For the Outback still has perils in its vast, eternal store!

SPINIFEX

(Much of the north and central parts of Australia's arid country is dominated by spinifex, of which there are about 50 species. Growing in clumps, and having pale green or yellowish-green spear-like leaves, it covers areas of sand or rocky plains for as far as the eye can see.
The spear shape of its leaves is an adaption to the fierce outback heat, for it helps reduce evaporation. Spinifex also has deep roots that tap the subterranean moisture, and its thick clumps provide homes, shelter and safety for much of our desert wildlife.
The species, Triodia irritans, *is commonly called 'porcupine grass' for fairly obvious reasons!*
The Reverend John Flynn, of 'Flynn of the Inland' fame, once called spinifex 'the wonder grass' because of its marvellous drought resisting qualities. Sometimes spinifex alone is all that keeps stock and wildlife alive.)

Spinifex! The very name brings thoughts of reddish sand;
Of arid plains and rocky hills throughout our mighty land;
Of kangaroos and emus; of endless, azure sky;
Of emptiness and silence; of summers, hot and dry;
Of dusty sheep and cattle; of camels, loose and lean;
Of Kimberleys and Uluru, and places in between.

There are many kinds of spinifex, but *Triodia irritans*
Is often the most common in the dry and desert sands.
It's seen in thickly-growing clumps from two to nine feet wide,
And often there is quite a crowd of animals inside!
Spiders, ants and silverfish, geckos, dragons, skinks,
Mulgaras, too, and hopping-mice, and many snakes, methinks!

There're many types of birds that eat the spinifex's seeds,
Finding them sufficient for their nutrimental needs.
Some birds need something extra, a juicy grub or two,
Or termites, ants and beetles, to mention just a few.
Pigeons, finches, bowerbirds - on spinifex they dine
Along with many parrots, a favourite of mine!

The spinifex, in times of drought, looks blackish to the eye,
A dead and useless plant it seems, its leaves completely dry.
But it's not dead, for all it needs is but an inch of rain,
And then, within a week or so, it's looking green again!
A tough and hardy plant, indeed, a plant that stays alive
When many others fade and die, unable to survive!

For lizards, birds and insects, and other creatures, too,
This spinifex is quite ideal, but not for me or you.
The plant looks comfortable enough, but gentle-looking leaves
Are not at all as they appear, their innocence deceives!
Sharp spines are in abundance, their pricking causing sores
On camels' legs, and horses', too, which owners can't ignore!

Spinifex will burn apace with heat that's quite intense,
With heavy, smoky columns, oily, black and dense.
It's good for boiling water for your mug of billy tea,
And, uproot a clump of spinifex, invert it, and you'll see
It makes a soft and springy bed; so, as the night hours pass,
Think kindly of the spinifex - Australia's 'wonder grass'!

SO YOU WANT TO KNOW MORE?

*(Whilst reading this book, you may have had some desire to know
something more about the Outback, that vast 'out there' of
Australia's inland.*
*This poem should give you some inkling of how to know more about
that vast and wonderful area we know as 'The Outback'.)*

So you want to see the Outback? You can visit it by train;
Take the railway up to Alice, then ride it back again.
You can look out from a window from an air-conditioned seat,
And drink your beer or coffee, and ignore the desert heat.
You may understand the vastness of the Outback as you see
The gidyea and the mulga and each small and stunted tree.
You may see the sand and gibber, and the red, far-distant range;
You may see the saltpans glaring, and watch the mirage change.
But you won't have seen the Outback in any depth at all,
You'll have seen a moving picture like a movie on the wall.

You can take a car or bus trip, drive through the desert dunes,
Sit by a creek at nightfall and watch the rising moon.
You can camp beside a billabong and hear the twilight sounds
As the creatures of the Outback scuffle gently on the ground.
You can see the tourist places - Stanley Chasm, Uluru,
(And they are great to visit, and I hope you see them, too!)
You can go and sit in silence in the middle of the scrub,
Or talk to local people in a little, outback pub.
But after you have driven for perhaps a month or more,
You'll have hardly scratched the surface of our great Outback,
      I'm sure!

You want to learn about the Outback? See how the Outback
     looks?
You can see some pretty pictures in some magazines or books.
You can read about its history, of life in earlier times,
You can read in prose and essay, and in ballads and in rhymes.
You can talk to other people who have lived out there for years,
And hear of their experience through laughter and through tears.
You can watch the television, see the Outback on the news,
Or watch a documentary of the Outback's marvellous views.
But you'll only know in theory of the Outback and its traits,
To really know the Outback you must learn another way.

To *really* know the Outback, you must live in it, my friend;
Feel the emptiness and silence where horizons never end.
Smell the faint and sweet aroma of the gentle, desert breeze;
And feel the deep frustration of the thunderclouds that tease
As they roar their mighty warnings, then slowly drift away,
Leaving dry and thirsty desert to survive another day!
Live through the fickle seasons, live through the drought and
          flood,
Live with the shifting sand-dunes, or metres deep in mud!
Discover, as you live there, the Aussie mateship true;
Then you'll start to know the Outback, and learn to love it, too!